The Bonniest Companie

Kathleen Jamie was born in the west of Scotland in 1962. Her poetry collection *The Tree House* won both the Forward Prize and the Scottish Book of the Year Award. *Mr and Mrs Scotland are Dead* was shortlisted for the 2003 International Griffin Prize. Kathleen Jamie's non-fiction books include the highly praised essay collections *Findings* and *Sightlines*. She teaches at Stirling University, and lives with her family in Fife.

Also by Kathleen Jamie

Poetry

The Overhaul

The Tree House

Jizzen

The Queen of Sheba

The Way We Live

Black Spiders

Non-fiction

Among Muslims

Findings

Sightlines

Kathleen Jamie

The Bonniest Companie

PICADOR

First published 2015 by Picador
an imprint of Pan Macmillan
20 New Wharf Road, London N1 9RR
Associated companies throughout the world
www.panmacmillan.com

ISBN 978-1-5098-0171-8

3 5 7 9 8 6 4 2

A CIP catalogue record for this book is available from the British Library.

Printed and bound by CPI Group (UK) Ltd, Croydon, CR0 4YY

Contents

Merle

The Bonniest Companie

The Bonniest Companie

Merle

The Shrew

Take me to the river, but not right now,
not in this cauld blast, this easterly
striding up from the sea
                    like a bitter shepherd –

and as for you, you Arctic-hatched, comfy-looking geese
                                        occupying our fields,
you needn't head back north anytime soon –

snow on the mountains, frozen ploughed clods –
weeks of this now, enough's enough

                              – but when my hour comes,
let me go like the shrew
right here on the path: spindrift on her midget fur,
                                        caught mid-thought, mid-dash

Glacial

A thousand-foot slog, then a cairn of old stones –
hand-shifted labour,
and much the same river, shining
                                        way below
as the Romans came, saw,
          and soon thought the better of.

Too many mountains, too many
                              wanchancy tribes
whose habits we wouldn't much care for
(but could probably match),
too much grim north, too much faraway snow.

Let's bide here a moment, catching our breath
and inhaling the sweet scent of whatever
                              whin-bush is flowering today

and see for miles, all the way hence
to the lynx's return, the re-established wolf's.

Merle

Thon blackbird in the briar
                    by the outfield dyke
doesn't know he's born
          doesn't know he's praise and part
of this Sabbath forenoon
                      north-Atlantic style.
From his yellow beak his song descends
                  to the year's first celandines;
his throat patters. With a yellow claw
he scarts his left lug

Soon the haar will burn off
         revealing the Rum Cuillin
happed in March snow, and the waters of the Minch
         but for now the blackie's
the centre of the world's eye
                  – till there! He's flown.

Thon Stane

Thon earthfast boulder by the bothy door,
taller than a man and
                    thrice as broad and
older than everyone put together –

stood there in his mossy boots
like he's just this very forenoon
                    wandered down the brae –

a chapman peddling bracken-besoms,
lichen-saucers
                    a few lampwicks of grass –

I open the door, though he gives no hawker's cry –
just proffers his mute wares,
                              as he has for long enough.

The Lighthouse

As good a climb as any, now the day's near done
                    the hill ahent the bothy –
a dry burn, then a basalt knuckle
like a throne,
            should you care to queen it
among shivery bracken
                    a wheen grazing sheep.

Already the Western Isles
lie dusty-pink along the horizon,
            and like a prodigal in a nightclub,
the Scalpay lighthouse
            keeps flashing its signature

three-white-every-twenty-second beam.

Deliverance

I'm waiting for the star to rise
– a planet maybe

that every evening tangles itself
in the still leafless branches

of the sycamore
framed by your smallest window

where it seems to flutter and tremble
like thon pied wagtail,

mind? trapped in a lobster-creel
on the pier at Elgol.

O fisherman's hand, reach in!
Send us chirruping!

The View

For too long I haven't
glanced at the sea
fully ten minutes!
– horizon shining like a magic key,
a whinny of spume at the cliff-foot,

and all the sky's silences, its dialects . . .

Now here comes a squall
all dressed in drab
bustling toward the mainland –
a smudge of rainbow
clutched like a shopping bag
in her right hand.

Eyrie I

I was feart we'd lost the falcons
and the falcons' eyrie
from the whinstone quarry back o the town
– their favoured plinth
                    vacant so long
grasses had raised
          thin flags over it, and winter rain
washed away their mutes,
but here she is! Conjured out of drizzle
and March mist, her yellow claws
a holdfast on the rock's edge –
                    her eye all-seeing
as she planes away again
over our rooftops and the firth.

The Ponies

Here they come, trotting
toward the bearers of kind words.

Beyond their field, the westernmost,
a rampart rises of cobble-stones and sea-weed,
then an ocean they'll never behold.

Tear down the fences!
Set the ponies free!

Till then, though
we name them for the fishing boats
tied up in the harbour:
the *Welcome Home*, the *Merlin*
– and this tough wee Sheltie
chewing, look! your sketch-book –
she is the *Radiant Queen*.

Corporation Road I

One night, in my father's arms
I was carried from our brick-built semi,
shown the stars above the steelworks' glare.

Corporation Road II

On my red swing I swept
high as its iron
chains allowed, the sky

I rushed toward disdained
to gather me; I birded up,
dizzied by its blue, its ungovernable clouds –

come back, said the Earth
I have your shadow.

The Heronry

6th Feb, a Saturday, I wheel the bike
out of its winter shed, go buy
papers and rolls
dump them on the kitchen table,
then cycle upriver on the south bank.
A dozen golden-eye
ride out by the channel marker, and
two-three tufted duck,
            but I want to check
if the herons are congregated yet,
scholarly and ridiculous,
in the spindly sauchs of the island,
                        though it's early days.
            That said, for the first time this year
the pylons of the Carse are shining
                        like someone somewhere's
flicked an almighty switch.

Eyrie II

That wind again, fit to flay you –
like pages snatched
clouds flit west,
with all that's written there, heartfelt, raw –
The street-lamps sift their small light down
on a wakeful street,
a slate slips, wheelie-bins coup
and three fields away, a branch
on a Scots pine snaps,
and down falls cradle and all.

What will the osprey do then, poor things
when they make it home?

Build it up, sticks and twigs –
big a new ane.

Soledades

Having lost my copy of Machado's *Soledades*, I search the garden. It's March,
blustery, daffodils nod, and already blossom's sprigging on next door's pear.
I've a hunch I left the book by the old railway sleeper that serves as a bench,
and further, that the same breeze as makes the frogspawn quiver
in our sandpit-turned-pond, as flaps the laundry, has snatched the book away.
And sure enough, it's there, tossed beneath the beech hedge and open
at a particular page, as though the breeze, riffling through, had spotted
his own name among the master's lines:

The deepest words

of the wise man teach us

the same as the whistle of the wind . . .

The Bonniest Companie

The Glen

April morning, rising mist,
last fugitive snow-drifts
cooried below the dykes' north sides,
a naked mountain
ash tree next a tumbling burn –
Ay, it's a different season here, different world . . .

So if you don't mind, heather of the hillside,
and it's alright by you, small invincible bird,
I'll lean on this here boulder
by the old drove road,
and get my eye in, lighting on this and that.

'It's nothing to us' you might shrug,
– and you'd be right.

Old Women

Thon tree,
earthfast at the foot
of your Alpine meadow,

dark, with mossy branches,
– apple perhaps –

can you give it a message?
Can you please say spring
will be there soon?

It's creeping up the mountain
as though carried on an old woman's back.

When we're old women
we will fetch spring too.

You know the tree I mean.

Wings Over New York

One of the Central Park
                    red-tailed hawks is
hunched in a leafless maple
pecking at a polythene bag.
When it flies its talons
                    entangle in the plastic
          so it plunges head down
                    – dreadful winged pendulum –
and everyone gasps,
          but with three strong wingbeats
it frees itself and soars
                    (*Where they nestin'?* someone asks,
I heard on Dakota, this year)
above the American Natural History Museum.

At the pondside hop hermit thrush,
fox- and swamp-sparrow
          and elsewhere in the Ramble
sounds a tiny NYPD siren
                    – a starling, high in a red oak.

Arbour

A sea-side arbour, a garden shanty,
knocked together out of driftwood and furnished
with a beat-up sofa
                    is where I sit,
striving to cultivate the strandline's

take-it-or-leave-it attitude, and happy to remain
till the last young blackbird
                          flies the nest
lodged in the dog-rose to my left.

From time to time father bird
hops across our common square of grass,
                                  cocking his head.
Friend, it's the sea you hear, vast and just
beyond those dunes, beyond your blackbird's ken,

but what do I know? May is again pegged out
across the whole northern hemisphere, and today
is my birthday. Sudden hailstones sting
this provisional asylum. We are not done yet.

The Garden

What little I know
of the way of the world
– scarce anything.
There's mystery in my own back green
– especially in my own back green!
Of drizzle
spangling the plum tree
the woodstack's shade,
the way a peanut-holder judders
when a speug's just flown –
and as for these daisies
encamped all over the grass
– same as last week's, last year's, same
yet not identical
to those I gazed at as a girl
candid and undemanding
all receiving their share

Blossom

There's this life and no hereafter –
                    I'm sure of that
but still I dither, waiting
for my laggard soul
to leap at the world's touch.

How many May dawns
                have I slept right through,
the trees courageous with blossom?
Let me number them . . .

I shall be weighed in the balance
                        and found wanting.
I shall reckon for less
                        than an apple pip.

The Hinds

Walking in a waking dream
I watched nineteen deer
pour from ridge to glen-floor,
then each in turn leap,
leap the new-raised
peat-dark burn. This
was the distaff side;
hinds at their ease, alive
to lands held on long lease
in their animal minds,
and filing through a breach
in a never-mended dyke,
the herd flowed up over
heather-slopes to scree
where they stopped, and turned to stare,
the foremost with a queenly air
as though to say: *'Aren't we*
the bonniest companie?
Come to me,
You'll be happy, but never go home.'

Ben Lomond

Thae laddies in the Celtic shirts,
a baker's dozen
lumbering all the way to the summit cairn
the hot last Saturday of May
as larks trilled
and the loch-side braes released their midgies . . .

Well, up at the raven-haunted trig-point
(as the sun shone bright o'er the whole lower Clyde)
they unfurled a banner,
and triumphant-sombre, ranked themselves behind it
for the photies,
'R.I.P.' it read, then the name of a wee boy

they'll never meet again. Ach,
would the wean were playing fit-ba
on some bonny banks somewhere . . .

There's no accounting for it, is there?
I mean the low road, and the high.

The Sheilings

Meeting no living creature
till the upper glen, where a few hinds
bounded away, I pitched my tent
on the emerald knoll
of a mossed-over sheiling hut. As the west-
facing hills dandied in the gloaming
and shadows filled the defiles, I fancied
I could hear the lasses of lang syne
ca'ing their kye, clattering pans, an infant's wail,
but the only sound was the Allt Ball a Mhulinn's
sweet-talk, which deepened
like a lover's, through the night.
What though, in June, is a night?
For a while the sky brooded, and once
a plane passed, high, heading south.

Solstice I

A late boat draws a wake upstream.
                                        A 90s anthem
– stadium rock – pulses from a neighbour's window,

while four or five gardens down
                                the reek of a bonfire rises
toward an overcast sky, dimming now
                                but for an amber swathe miles long,
west-north-west above the Sidlaws.

Daylight's at full reach, and still has business here,
or so it thinks –
                but the town's swifts are hid
                                        under their mysterious eaves
and it's gey near midnight. Then it's over –
midsummer: one fewer of our portion,
                                                one less left in the jar.

MIGRATORY

The Cliff

Let's take our chances here with the mortal,
the common and the mortal,
and stroll among the clifftop
drifts of pink thrift,
the throat-catching fulmar-shit updraft
and let space open
between word and world
wind-strummed, trembling

A Turn in a Stair

Tree with dark limbs
twelve or thirteen
stone steps up
between houses shuttered and locked –

tree with leaves like spearheads
shader and protectress
where the alley turns –

you're familiar, like a picture
I feared in a book
long years before
finding myself lost
on the Carrer de Pedro Sebastian
and climbing toward you

tree with white flowers

The Stair

Nana you are not there, no
hale in body behind the black door but
here I come coiling up the stair wi my paper
poke of Jujubes and the *Beezer*. Two landings

first then yours. I dart whippit-quick
past the toilet at the turn
in case there's an auld
                    bogeyman hiding. Stone

gassy smell and it's twenty odd
                    years since the war, but
naebody's bothered to scrape the black-out paint
off the stair-heid window. Oh this was a bleak land then.

Nana will you not be there
                    in the room and kitchen?
Here's my fingernail, scratching a peephole to keek through.

The Girls

A summer evening,
                              a rubber ball
thumped against a harled
1950s gable wall

– and pitched between
chant and song,
our lasses' rhyme: *plainy, clappy,*
roll-a-pin – as we practised

birling round so quick
we caught the same ball
bingo! on its rebound – alive

to its arc and Earth's spin
as the gloaming deepened
and one by one, we were called in.

The Missing

When the wee girl toddled round the corner
                                        into our street,
we quit our hidey-seek
and hunkered level with her
oddly drooping eyes. She was no-one's
                              baby sister that we knew.
Was she crying? Maybe. Anyhow
her pants were soaked, so we pulled them off,
left them in the gutter, tugged down her yellow frock,

then gripping a small hand each, me and Sandra McQueen
set off with her,
                    back toward McColl's and the Co-op
– where else could she have wandered from?

Big girls, we knew the way
                                   or so we thought
but the road, in its summer haze,
only seemed to lengthen, lengthen, lengthen, the more we walked.

The Piper

Though feart of the river
            and its dying goldfish smell,
I dared once go
slithering upstream from the tannery

with Neil and Tommy Hunter
                                    and the Laidlaw girls.
We wanted to see for ourselves
the embankment and bricked-up tunnel
where centuries ago,
                      – or so Neil said –
a piper had went marching in.

For miles, they heard his pipes play
under the hills
                        – until they ceased
then nothing more

that day to this: a gang of bairns
ankle deep in ancient water, asking
                        D'you believe? How do you no believe?

World Tree

What kind of a tree was yon, stationed
like a beggar at the bottom of our lane
where we braved on scooters and wee bikes?

It marked our world's end, maimed,
relic-grey, down past the last back gate
where the fields began,
growing from before they built the scheme.

That was where we hunkered,
from infancy till the gloamings of our teens,
knees drawn up to our chins, whispering
sweet horrors . . .
                    Crone-tree, tribal-root,
I haven't thought of you in years, your sap
in me, but wonder now what kind you were
– elder or hawthorn, bour or may
                    – and why I suddenly care.

Fianuis

Well, friend, we're here again,
          sauntering the last half-mile to the land's frayed end
to find what's laid on for us, strewn across the turf –
gull feathers, bleached shells,
                    a whole bull seal, bone-dry,
knackered from the rut
(we knock on his leathern head, but no-one's home).

Change, change – that's what the terns scream
                    down at their seaward rocks
fleet clouds and salt kiss –
everything else is provisional,
                    us and all our works.
I guess that's why we like it here.
               Listen: a brief lull,
                    a rock pipit's seed-small notes.

Migratory I

Mind that swan? The whooper we found
neck slack on the turf, head pointing north like a way-sign,
how you stooped and opened its wing?
                                        I paid scant heed
to your naming of parts: *coverts, ulna, primaries*
being scunnert with the place, its gales and sea-roar
– but this wing – this was a proclamation!
The wind-fit, quartz-bright power of the thing! A radiant gate
one could open and slip through . . .
We dragged the swan to the lee of an old dyke
tucked it in neat, a white stone,
then trudged up out of the glen. At the ridge
again, we got clouted properly,
                    staggered on, half elated, half scared.

The Berries

When she came for me
through the ford, came for me
through running water
I was oxter-deep in a bramble-grove
glutting on wild fruit. Soon
we were climbing the same
sour gorge the river fled, fall
by noiseless fall. I mind
a wizened oak
cleaving the rock it grew from,
and once, a raptor's mewl.
Days passed – or what passed for days,
and just as I'd put the whole misadventure
down to something I ate,
she leapt twice, thrice, my sick
head spun, and here we were:
a vast glen ringed by snow-peaks,
sashaying grass, a scented breeze,
and winding its way toward us
that same world-river –
its lush banks grazed by horses, horses
I knew she'd leave me for,
right there, her own kin –
no use my pleas, no use
my stumbling back down
to where the berries grew,
because this is what I wanted,
so all I could do was brace myself
and loosen my grip from her mane.

23/9/14

So here we are,
dingit doon and weary,
happed in tattered hopes
(an honest poverty).
Wir flags are wede awa,
the withered leaves o shilpit trees
blaw across deserted squares,
and the wind
– harbinger of winter –
quests round the granite statues
– and so on and etcetera.
We ken a' that. It's Tuesday. On wir feet.
Today we begin again.

Homespun

Migratory II

eftir Hölderlin

As the burds gang faur
he luiks aye aheid
the prince o them, and caller

agin his breist
blaws aa he meets wi
i the heich,
                    the quate o the lift

but ablo, his braw lands
lie bienly shinin

– and flittin wi him: hauflins
ettlin for the furst time
tae win furrit

but wi cannie wing-straiks,
he lowns thaim

Migratory III

Those swans out there at the centre of the loch
a dozen or thirteen
moored close together, none adrift –
they've only just arrived
an arrow-true, close-flocked, ocean-crossing skein,

and bone-weary, sleep now
heads under wings,
so darkness can restore them,
though darkness is what they've just flown.

None today is the Watcher, none the Vigilant One,
scanning the rushes of the shore
for a few notes of movement,
a fox, say, or a lad they recall
thousands of years ago
skulking in a skin boat with his broken flute
and pockets filled with sling-stones.

High Water

When the tide returns
from its other life,
bearing its adulterer's gifts

and the wrack-plastered reef
becomes again a sunk unknown,

then we should take our leave –
steering between the telegraph poles
that mark safe channel,

and all the lives we never lived
piled behind us on the shore.

Let them anguish over that! Offspring,
lost friends, our mystified lovers'
sad cries fading in our ears

till the next tide brings us bobbing
back home again – us,
and our shamefaced boat.

Homespun

The yellow-shaded lamp
                    squat on a table
in our mother's corner of the living-room
was made by us, from an empty
Dimple whisky bottle
                    meshed in faux-gold wire,
and crowded to the neck with dog whelks or buckies
picked up from the beach at –
                                        was it Brodick?
I can feel yet the itch of the green/
brown-flecked hand-knit I wore
            rapt on that seashore
                              gathering shell after shell.
What happened to that
                    – the lamp, and all the stitch-work
it shone upon
                    squandering no light?

Scotland's Splendour

At the back of our local charity shop's
a book I last recall
crammed into my bedside cabinet
among the *Beano* annuals and the *Broons*.
Its cover photo shows a river
racing from snow-crisped hills,
a bridge, a whitewashed byre,
scenery so familiar I open it,
and rediscover in 'full natural colour'
page after page of mountains
mirrored in placid lochs,
cattle ambling by reedy lochs,
stags on heather-moor
and one modern silver cataract:
the spillway of a new-built hydro dam.
All this, I'd been given to understand,
was 'Scotland', a gift sent down
during our sojourn among the southron
but too young to read, I'd simply
pored over its rowan-trees,
cottages, castle-crowned rocks,
hen-wives wearing woollen coats,
ferry boats in the gloaming. How odd
to feel its weight once more,
that hardback nation
which declared itself in our speech
– ours were the grey-rain tones of Clyde-built

trams and cranes (illustrated on p19)
– a dream-tinged land we pick up,
then shelve again, a place
so difficult and faraway
I grat miserable tears the day
my folks announced we were flitting,
turning north again,
back to thon unknown cold stone 'home'.

Wings Over Scotland

Glenogil Estate: poisoned buzzard (Carbofuran).
No prosecution.
Millden Estate: poisoned buzzard (Alphachloralose).
No prosecution.
Millden Estate: poisoned golden eagle 'Alma' (Carbofuran).
No prosecution.
Glenogil Estate: poisoned white-tailed eagle '89' (Carbofuran).
No prosecution.
'Nr Noranside': poisoned red kite (Carbofuran).
No prosecution.
Glenogil Estate: poisoned buzzard (Chloralose).
No prosecution.
Glenogil Estate: poisoned pigeon bait (Carbofuran).
No prosecution.
Millden Estate: shot buzzard.
No prosecution.
Rottal & Tarabuckle Estate: dead kestrel
inside crow cage trap. **No prosecution.**
'Nr Bridgend': remains of buzzard
found under a rock. Suspicious death.
'Nr Noranside': remains of buzzard
found beside pheasant pen. Suspicious death.
Millden Estate: satellite-tagged golden eagle
caught in spring trap, then apparently uplifted
overnight and dumped on Deeside.
No prosecution.
Glen Esk: Disappearance of sat-tagged red kite.
No other transmissions or sightings of bird.

The Storm

Mind thon wild night
                how the pair of us
got lost, and clung together, stumbled on
                        scared half daft
by a wraith-like moaning through the mirk
till we found its source:
                just a metal gatepost
with a voice the storm had loaned?
– A post we knew: it showed
the path to the croft-house
                        we'd rented cheap
till spring at least, when we went our separate ways.

Mind too what we told each another
                            that far-off day?
Be brave:
by the weird-song in the dark you'll find your way.

The Tradition

For years I wandered hill and moor
Half looking for the road
Winding into fairyland
Where that blacksmith kept a forge

Who'd heat red hot the dragging links
That bound me to the past,
Then, with one almighty hammer-blow
Unfetter me at last.

Older now, I know nor fee
Nor anvil breaks those chains
And the wild ways we think we walk
Just bring us here again.

Autumn

O whence the leaves
scuttering down Easter Road,
sycamore and rowan
desperate as refugees,
crowding against the wheels of street-side dumpsters
– common leaves
with two–three crisp packets, like gaudy imposters
fleeing by outside the corner-shop
convenient for milk and pornography . . .

see the leaves hurry, *Shy but Dirty* –
past the Chinese nail-bar,
Mr Greg's Tattoos –
they're here, look:
blown into your stair
with the pizza delivery leaflets . . .
O whither the leaves?

Another You

That Sixties song on the radio tonight
shrank me right down
eye-level with the raffia-faced,
Bush-made wireless
hunkered on the sideboard
in our family semi. If I could
spell out its Old World names,
backlit with a wartime glow:
Moscow, Oslo, Berlin,
it's because you'd taught me:
holding up flash-cards
with *LOOK LOOK,*
printed in cheerful font,
making me sound out loud
the OO, then the Kuh
that stood, also, for *Kathleen,*
and the only song I ever
heard you sing – Joseph Locke's
'I'll take you home again, Kathleen'
which aye made me greet. Well
that old Seekers thing
sure took me home again:
Dad's chair, sofa, ornaments,
your knitting bag, all
needles and pins. Sometimes
I tried on your specs,
the ones kept among the yarn

and reserved for 'close work'.
Wearing them sent my look-or-seek
haywire: the sideboard loped,
the carpet yawed,
– but you'd snatch them back,
claiming I'd ruin my eyes.
'Close work' was your pride;
you'd steered the satin
of your own wedding dress
under the Singer's clamped-down foot;
our grey school jerseys purled
onto your lap. Even I had my uses:
hands outstretched, I'd tension
skeins of wool for you to wind;
and grew, as I grew, to relish
the brush of your inch-tape
against my skin,
arms-length was as close as we got.
But I was wee and loved
the wireless's valves'
hot-dust smell, the steam-iron,
gas-fire; warmly clad we were,
if rarely hugged –
love was a primary seven
dance dress you sewed for weeks,
a florid pinafore I wore
but once, then took scissors to –
not in malice, more in hope
that I too might magic
some transformation, from girlish frock

to the longed-for elegance
of a maxi skirt – a crime,
when you discovered it,
I couldn't explain. I never
could explain myself, never
could explain. But that old number
swelling through my kitchen
this dark November night
moves me dearly. It's seven years
since you died, and suddenly I know
what the singers say is true –
that seek as I might, I'll never
find another you. But that's alright.

Solstice II

Here comes the sun
summiting the headland – pow!
straight through the windows of the 10.19
– and here's us passengers,
splendid and blinking
like we're all re-born,
remade exactly, and just where we left off:
the students, the toddler, the tattoo'd lass,
the half dozen roustabouts
headed off-shore
cracking more beers and more jokes.
Angus at midwinter
or near as makes no odds –
faint shadows raxed
over fields of dour earth,

every fairmer's fenceposts
splashed with gold.

Gale

Whit seek ye here?
There's noucht hid i' wir skelly lums
bar jaikies'nests.

Notes and Acknowledgements

Merle – A merle is a blackbird. This book began in earnest with a week's residency at Sweeny's Bothy on the Isle of Eigg. Many thanks to the Bothy Project, and to Lucy Conway and Eddie Scott.

The Hinds – I had in mind the last verses of the old ballad Tam Lin, when the Queen of the Fairies rages against Janet, saying: 'She has ta'en awa the bonniest knight/in a' my companie.'

World Tree – Bour-tree is Scots for elder, may is hawthorn.

Fianuis – Say *Fee-ah-nish*. The north-running peninsula on the Hebridean island of North Rona.

23/9/14 – In 2014 I strove to write a poem a week. Those poems became this book. The Scottish independence referendum was held on 18/9/14.

Migratory II – A fragment by Friedrich Hölderlin (1770–1843) translated into English by Michael Hamburger:

> As slowly birds migrate/ He looks ahead/ The prince, and cooly blows/ Against his breast all he meets with when/ There's silence round about him, high/up in the air, but richly shining below him/ Lies his estate of regions, and with him, for/ The first time seeking victory, are the young/ But with his wingbeats/ He moderates.

Migratory III – There have been discovered Palaeolithic flutes, 30,000 years old, made from swans' bones.

Wings Over Scotland – A 'found' poem, alas.
https://raptorpersecutionscotland.wordpress.com/

Thanks are due to the editors of magazines and journals where some of these poems first appeared: *The London Review of Books, Irish Pages, New Statesman, Poetry Review.*

I was fortunate enough to be given the 2015 Mark Ogle Award. 'The Sheilings' was written to that.

A version of 'The Glen' was commissioned by the Bristol Festival of Ideas as part of their New Lyrical Ballads project.

Very special thanks are due to Olivia Lomenech Gill for her cover artwork. Seeing her finished work was like looking into my own soul.